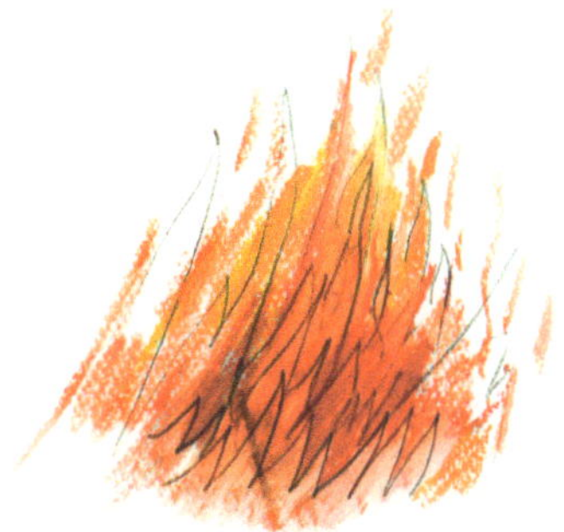

"So, like a forgotten fire, a childhood can always flare up again within us."

—Gaston Bachelard
Philosopher

HORN OF PLENTY

A LOST & FOUND IMAGINATION

WRITTEN & ILLUSTRATED BY

Shamona Stokes

Once there was a shy little creature of the forest named Ooni.
It was brightly colored with iridescent spots that changed in the light.

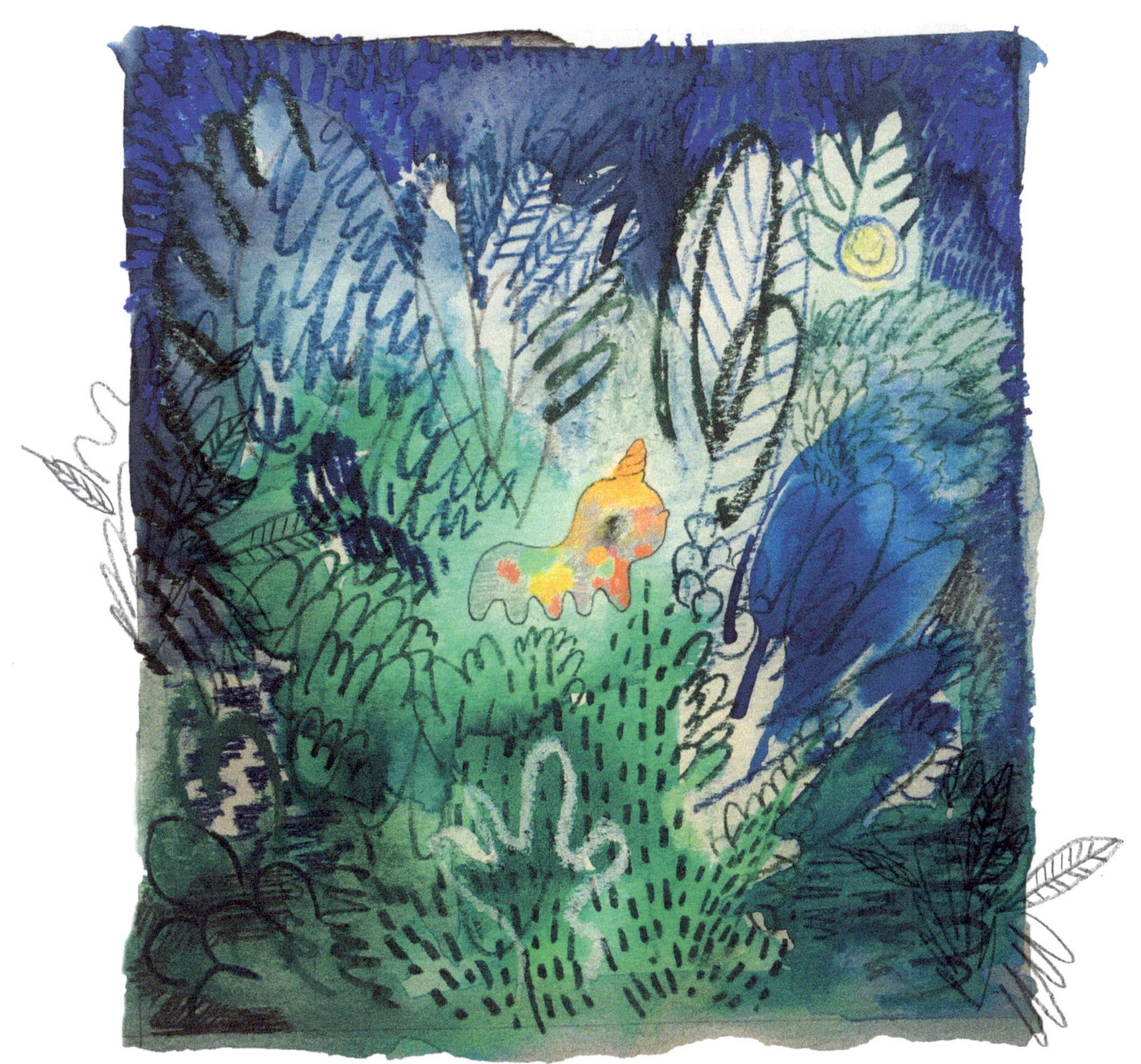

On its crown was a small horn that dreamed and imagined.

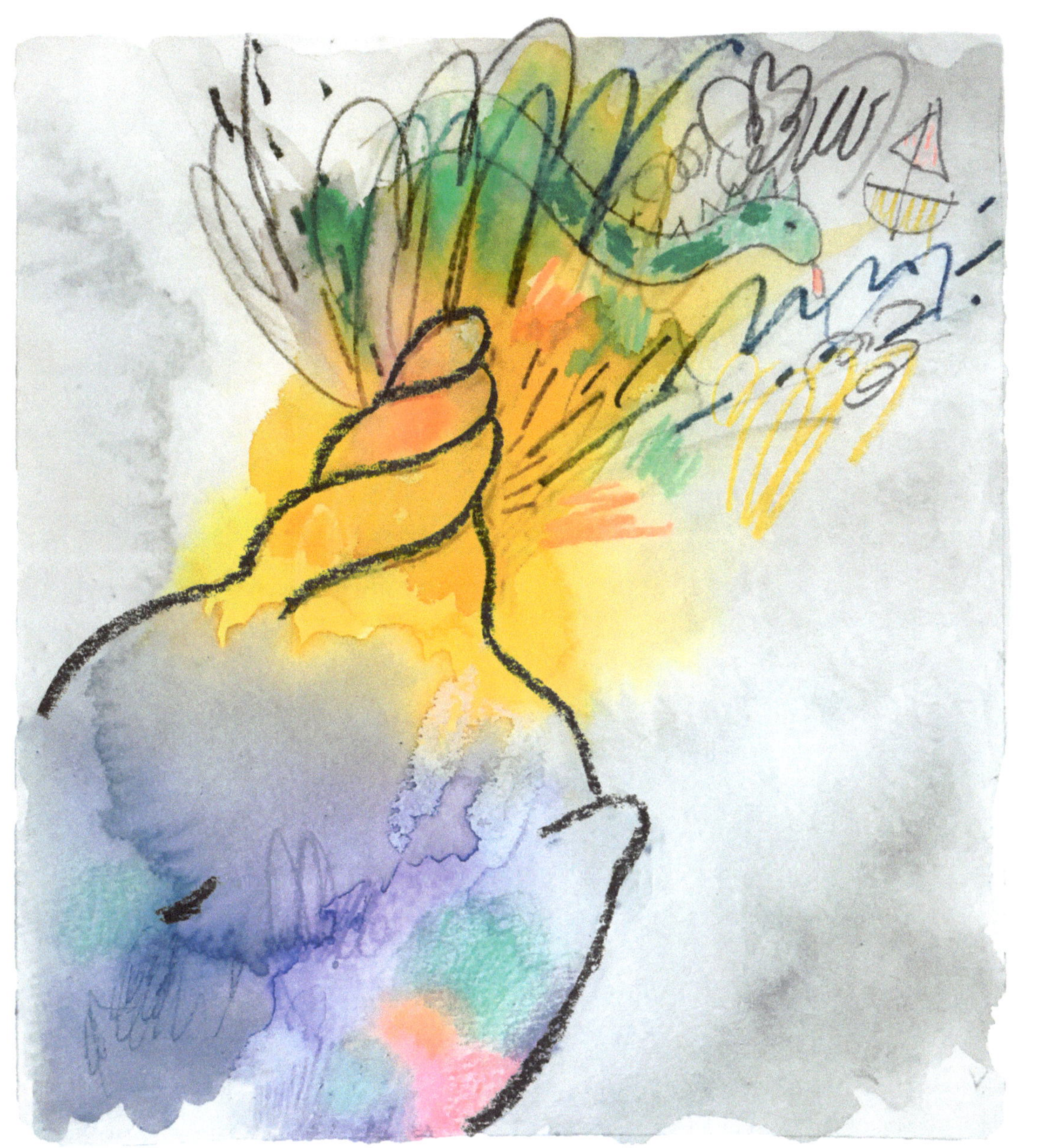

Ooni created the thingies that it had dreamed up.
There was no point to it really—other than just playing and being happy.

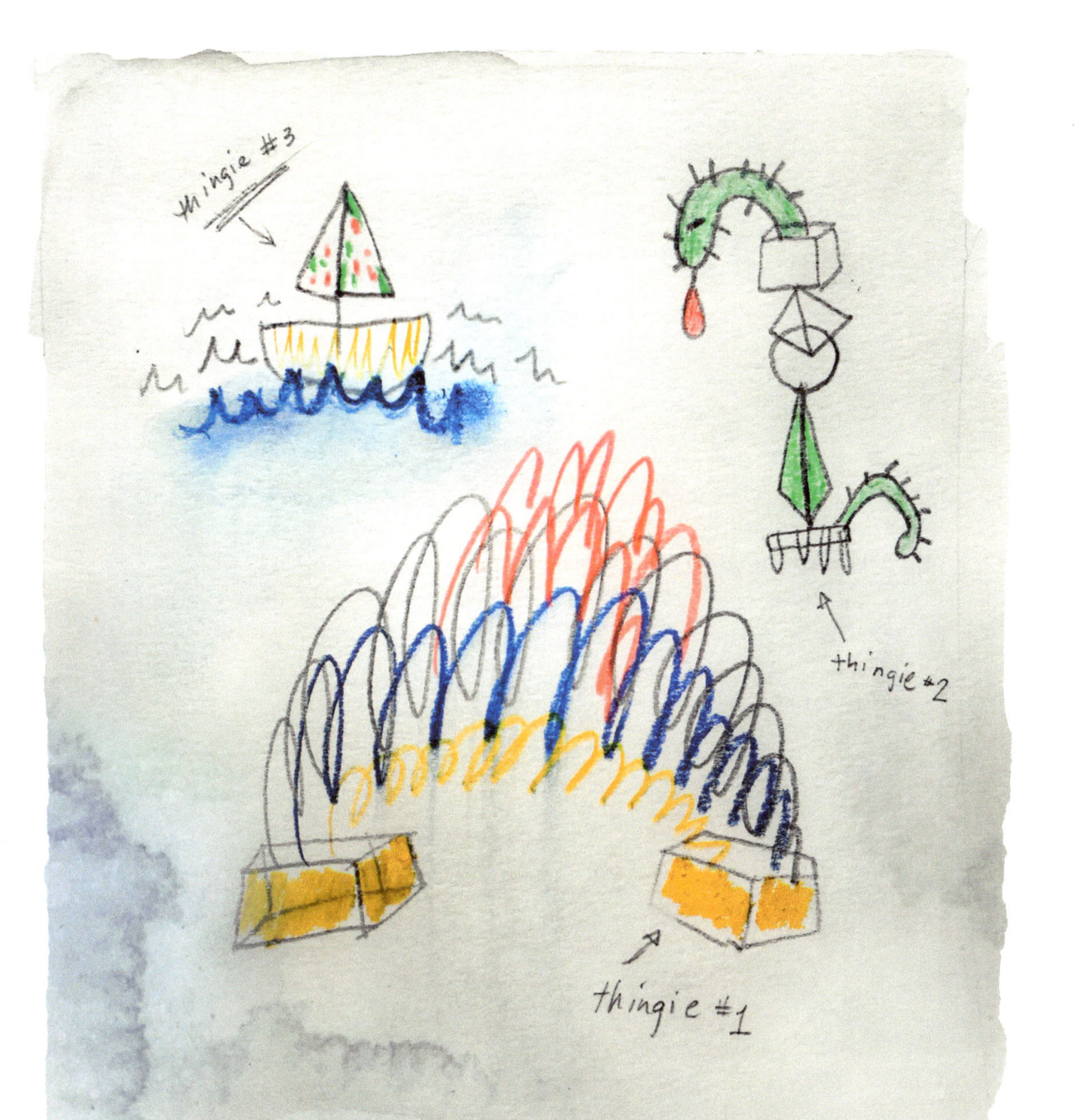

thingie #3
thingie #2
thingie #1

Peering out of the forest one day, Ooni noticed some other creatures!
Did they make thingies too? Maybe they'd want to be friends?!

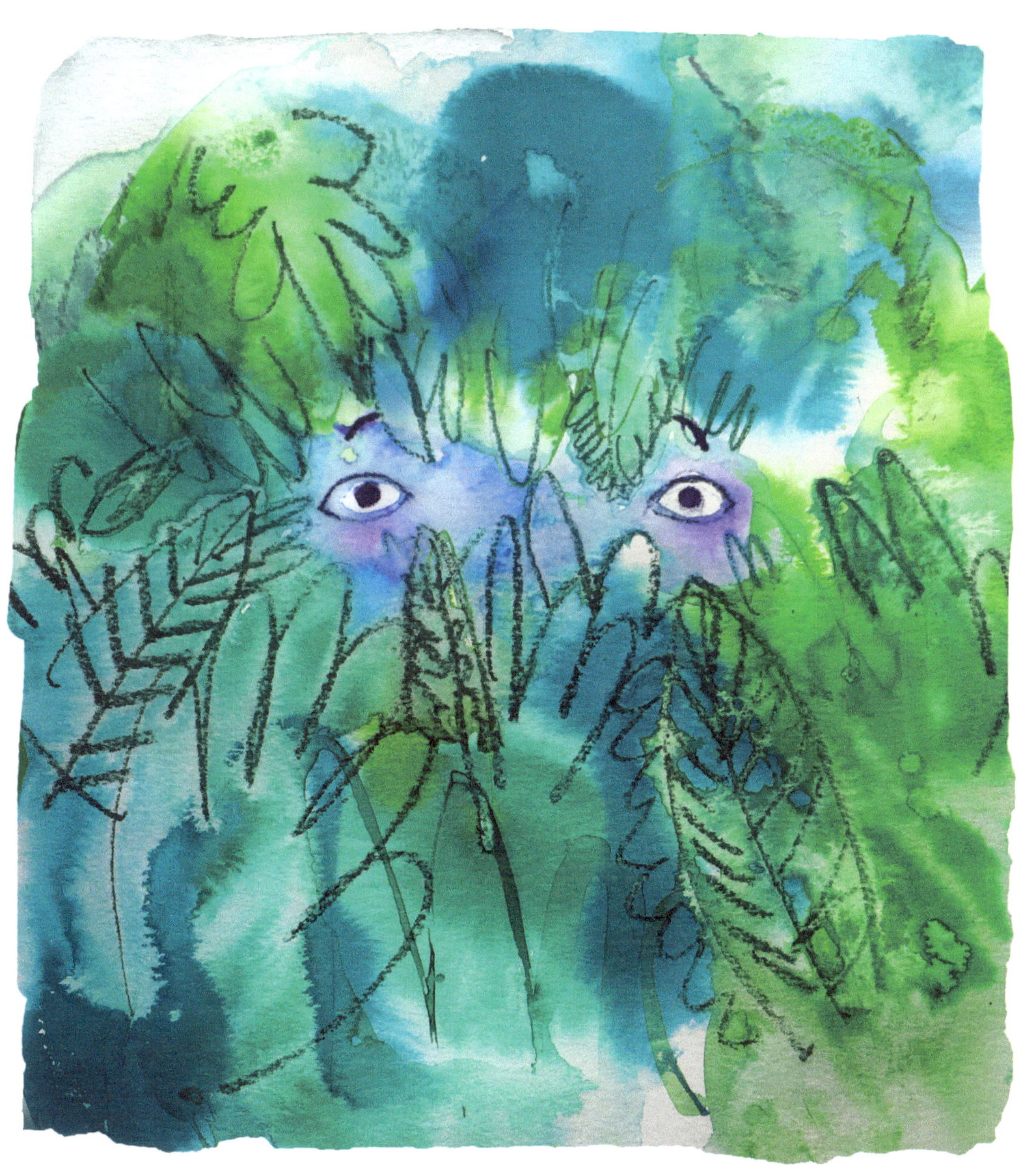

The timid creature worked up the courage to befriend the others,
but they made fun of Ooni's strange spots and horn.

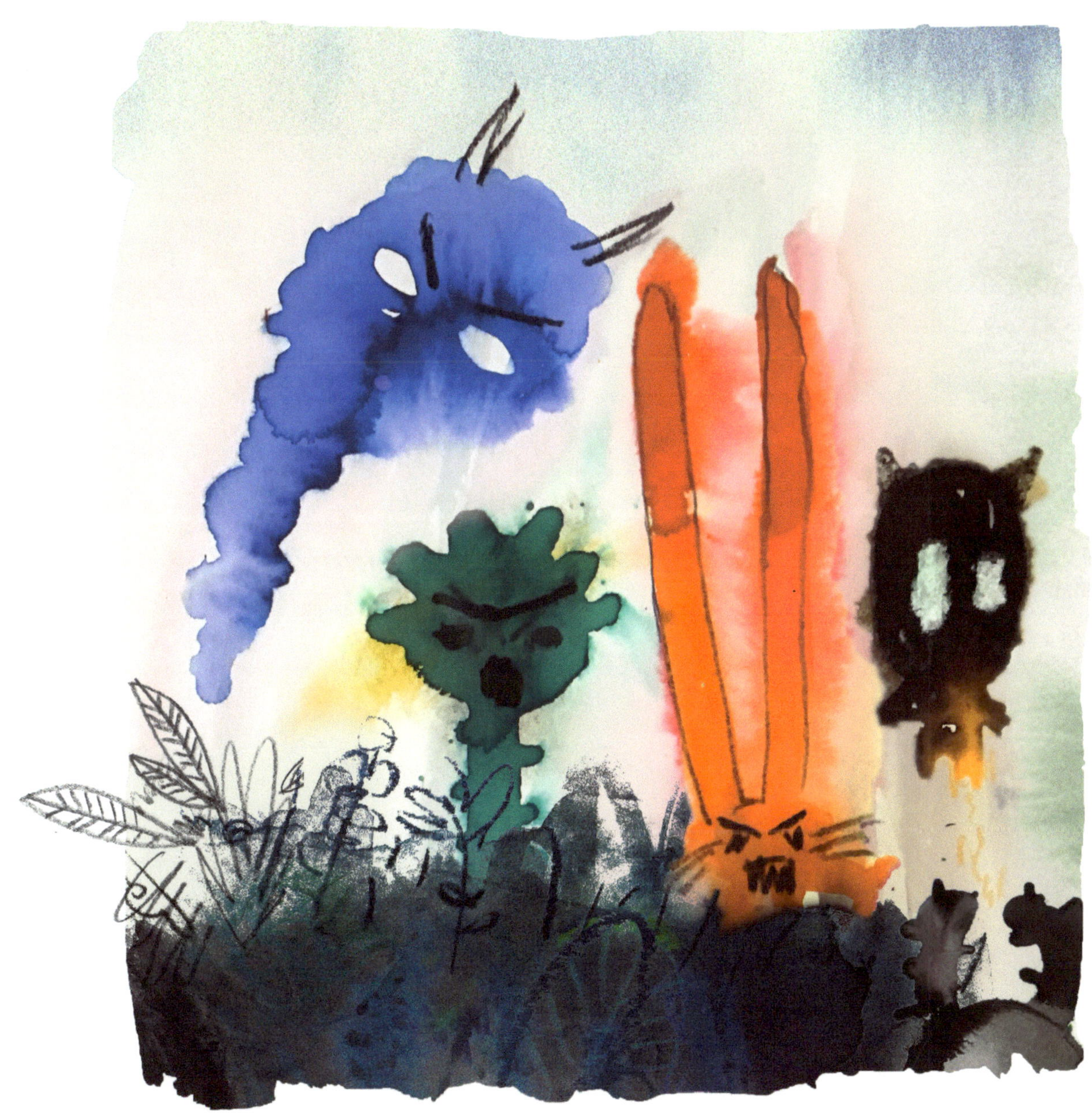

Then they ignored Ooni.
Which was worse, it wondered—to feel ashamed or to feel invisible?

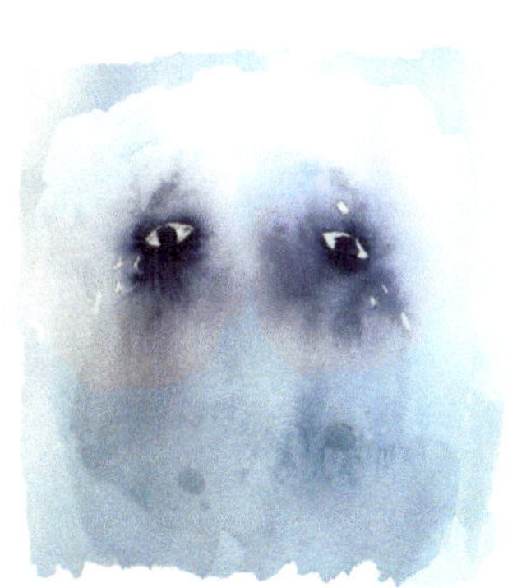

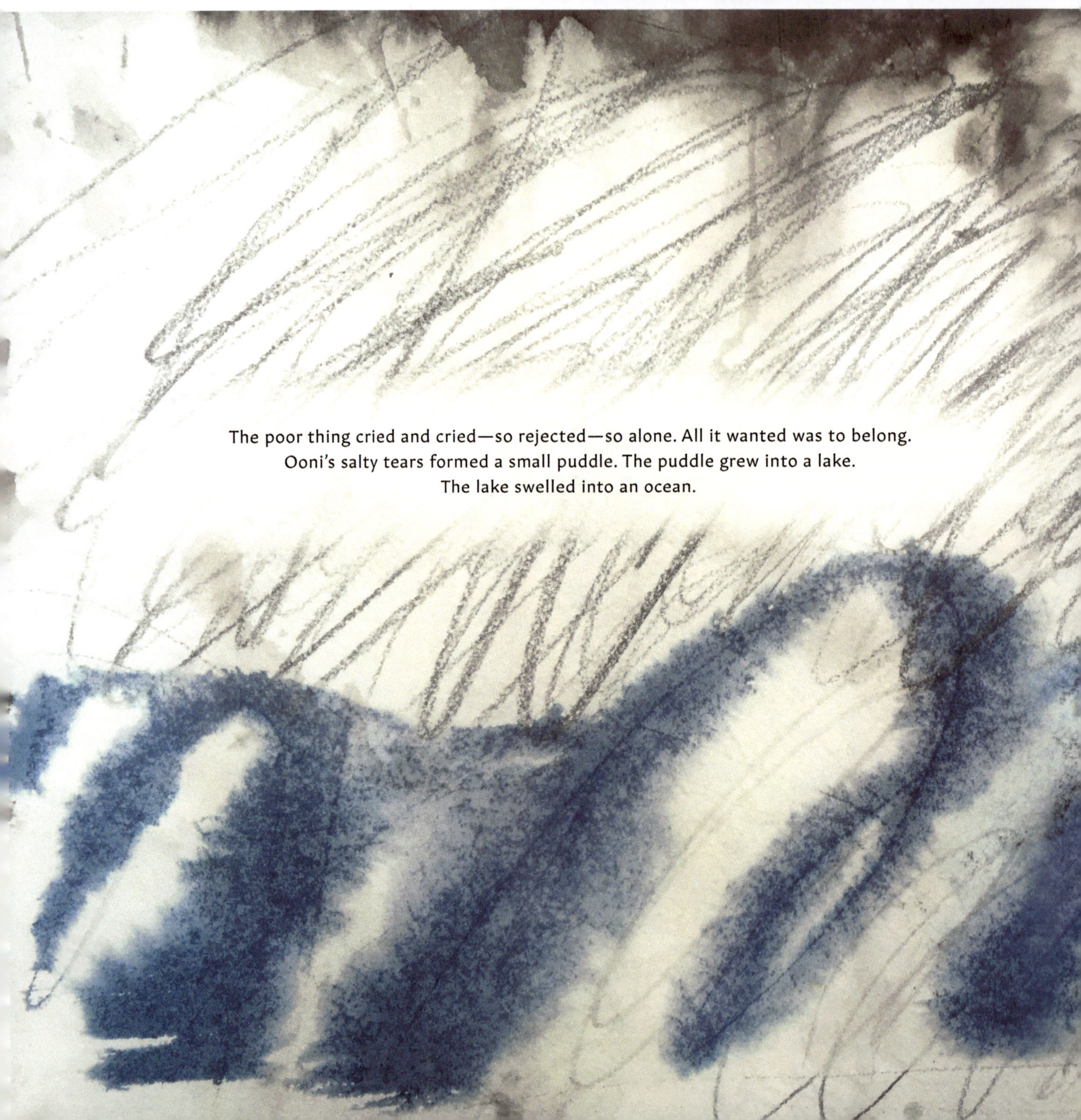

The poor thing cried and cried—so rejected—so alone. All it wanted was to belong.
Ooni's salty tears formed a small puddle. The puddle grew into a lake.
The lake swelled into an ocean.

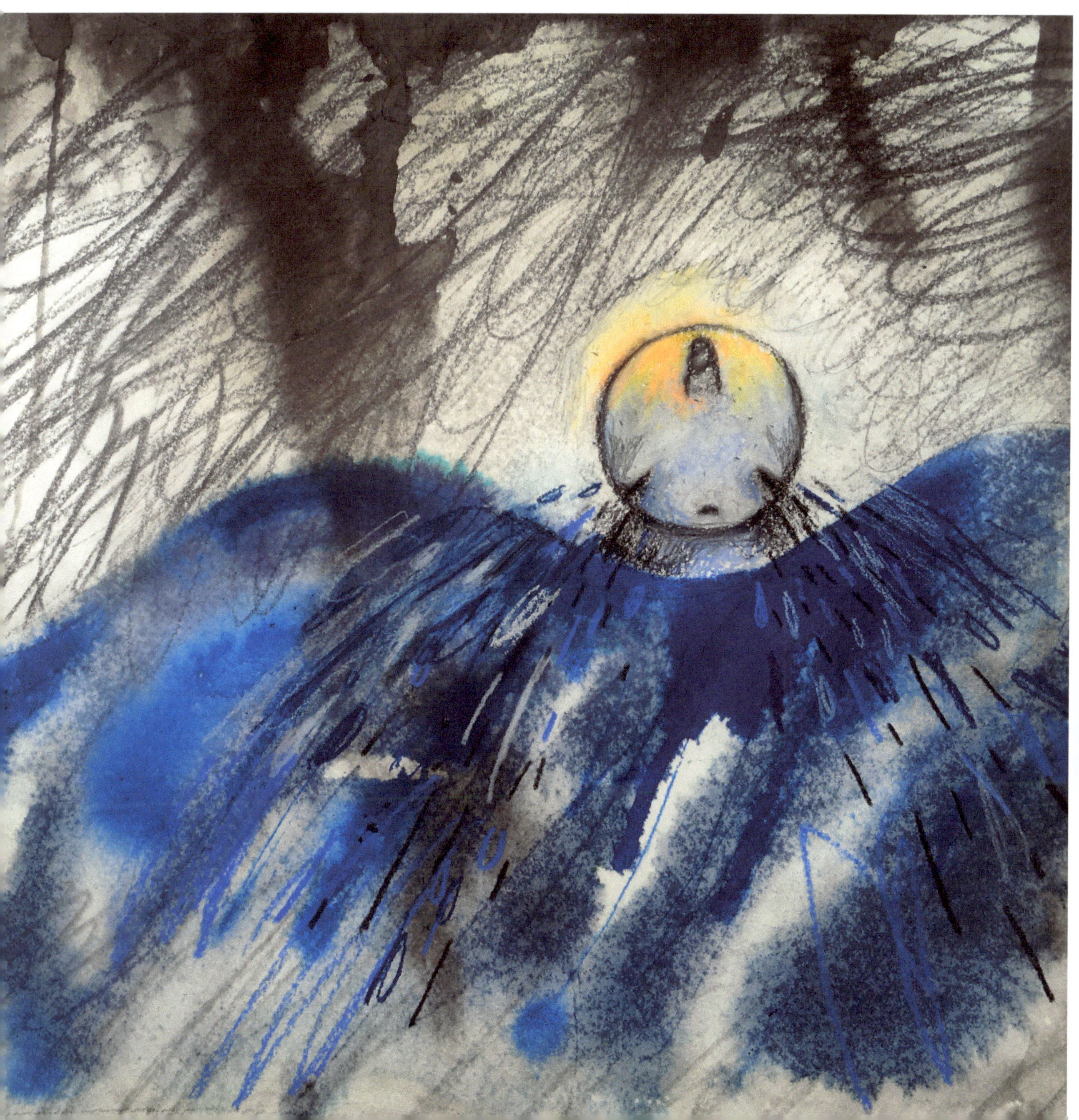

"I hate this stupid horn!" it yelled. Ooni crawled onto dry land, plucked the horn from its crown, and threw it into the sea. Its bright colors faded to gray.

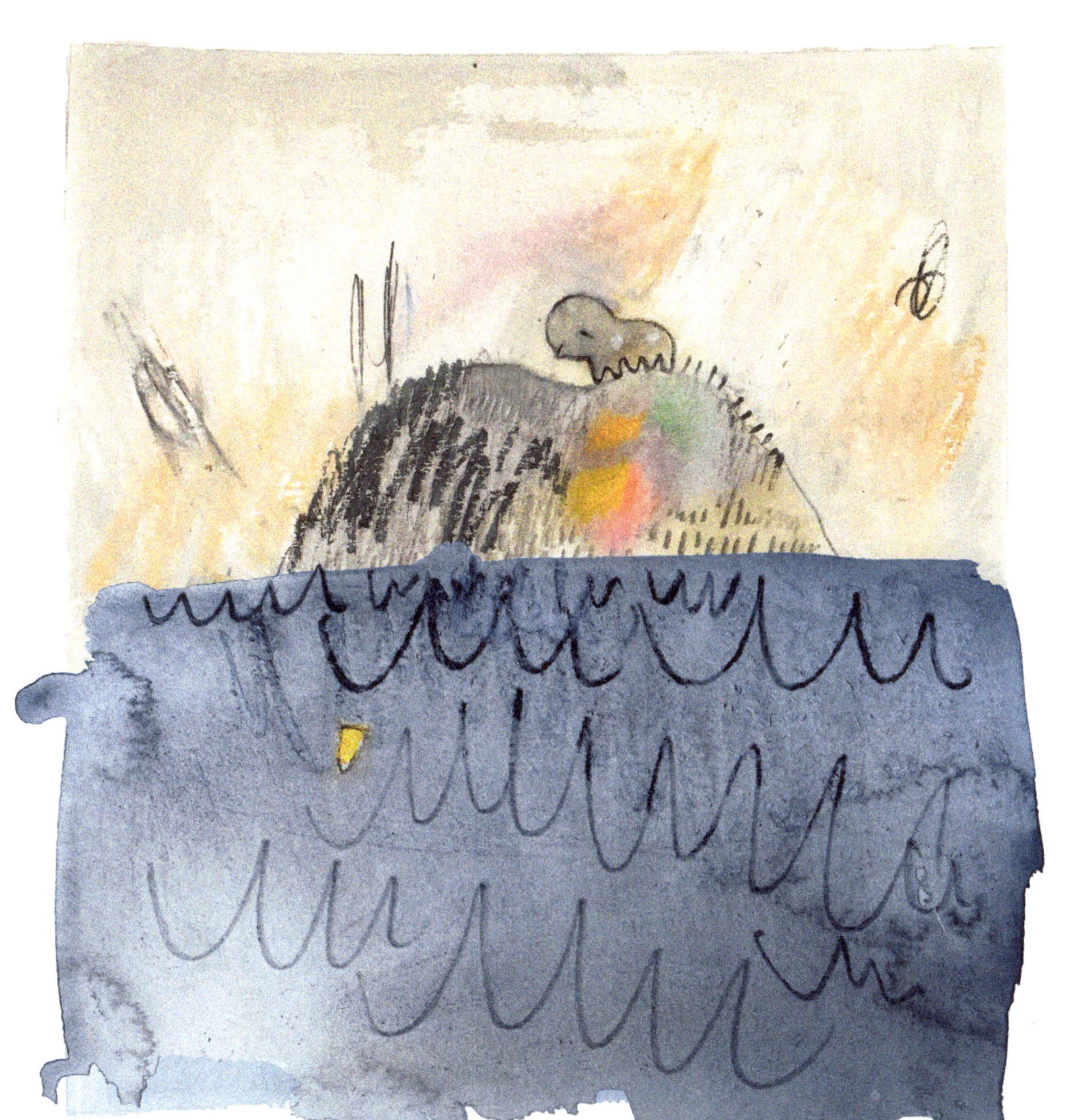

The sea of tears evaporated into a shaggy cloud that followed Ooni everywhere...
always overhead, casting a shadow.

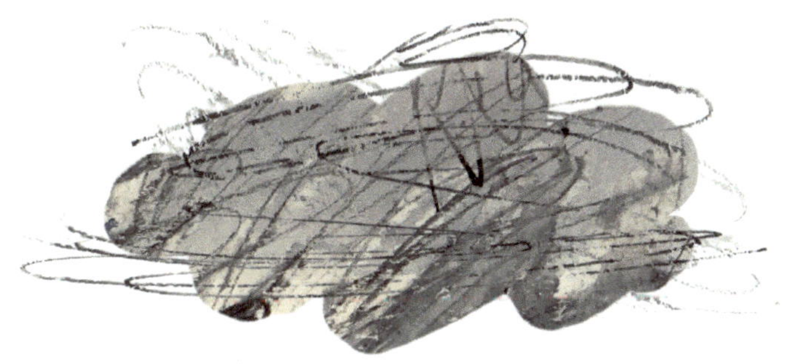

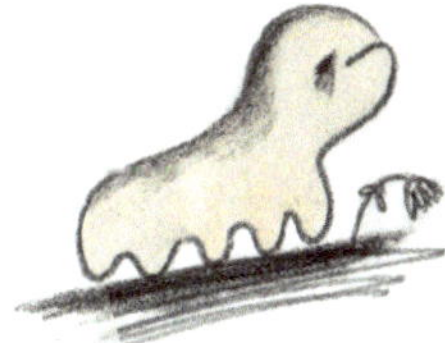

The cloud grew bigger and bigger. Darker and darker.
Until one day, it was SO big and the thunder was SO loud that it could not be ignored.

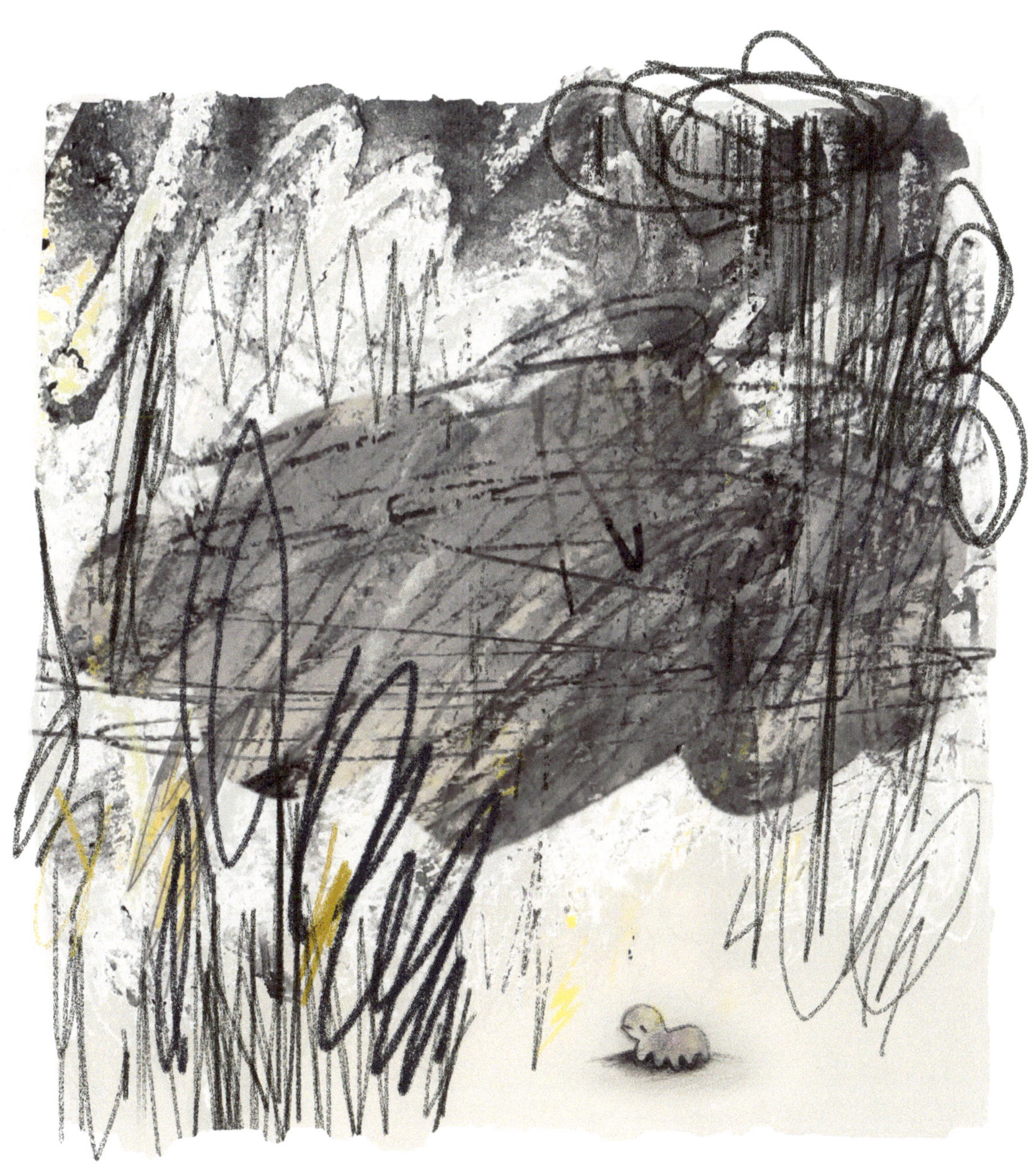

The cloud spit out a stormy thunderbolt that stopped Ooni dead in its tracks.
"Ouch!" it yelped, as the bolt struck its bare head. It collapsed into darkness.

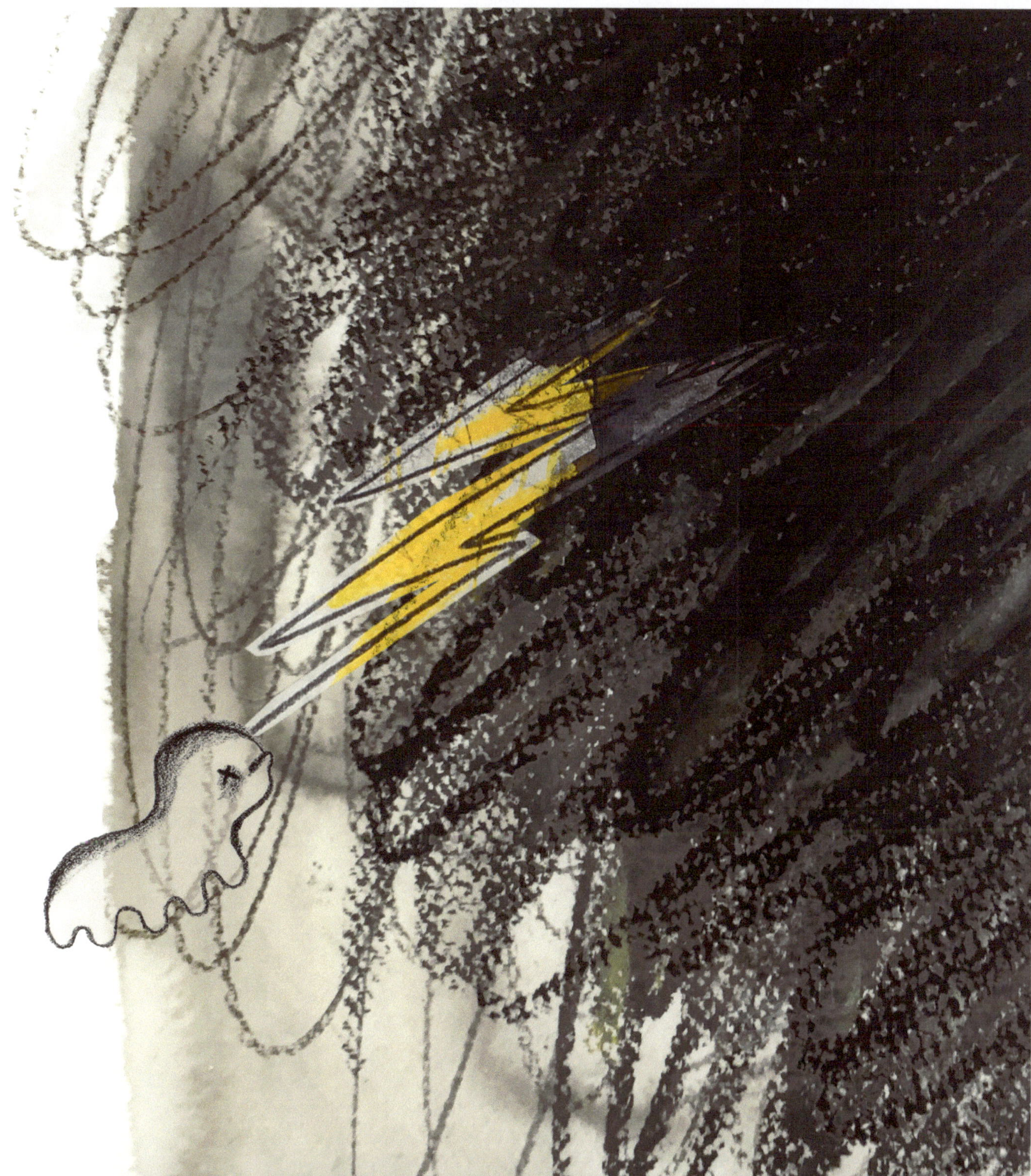

The days passed, and Ooni slept.
It felt safe and protected as the colors of warmth blanketed it.

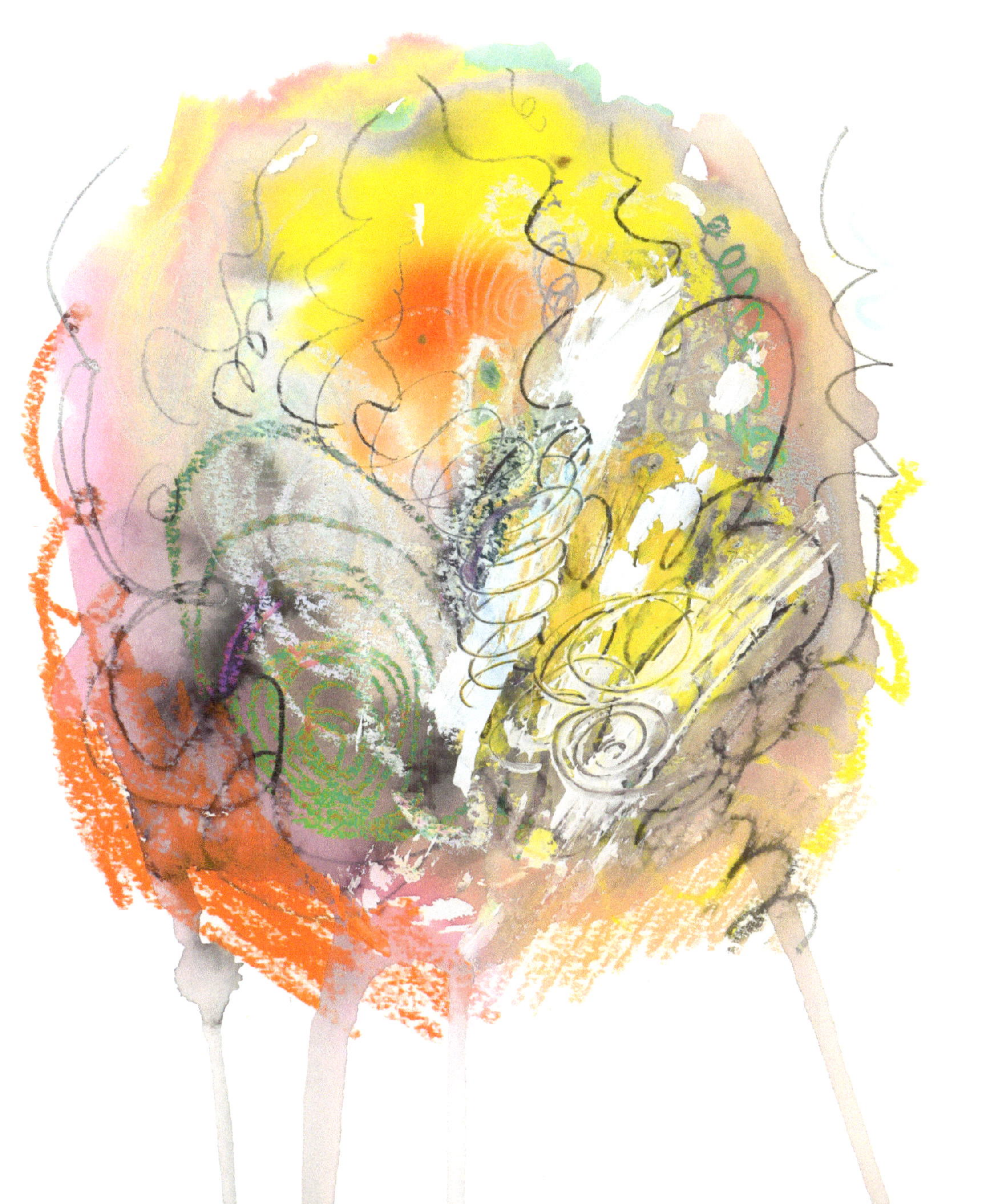

After much time had passed, Ooni finally emerged from its resting place and walked outside.
It looked back and saw the soft cocoon that it had spun for itself.

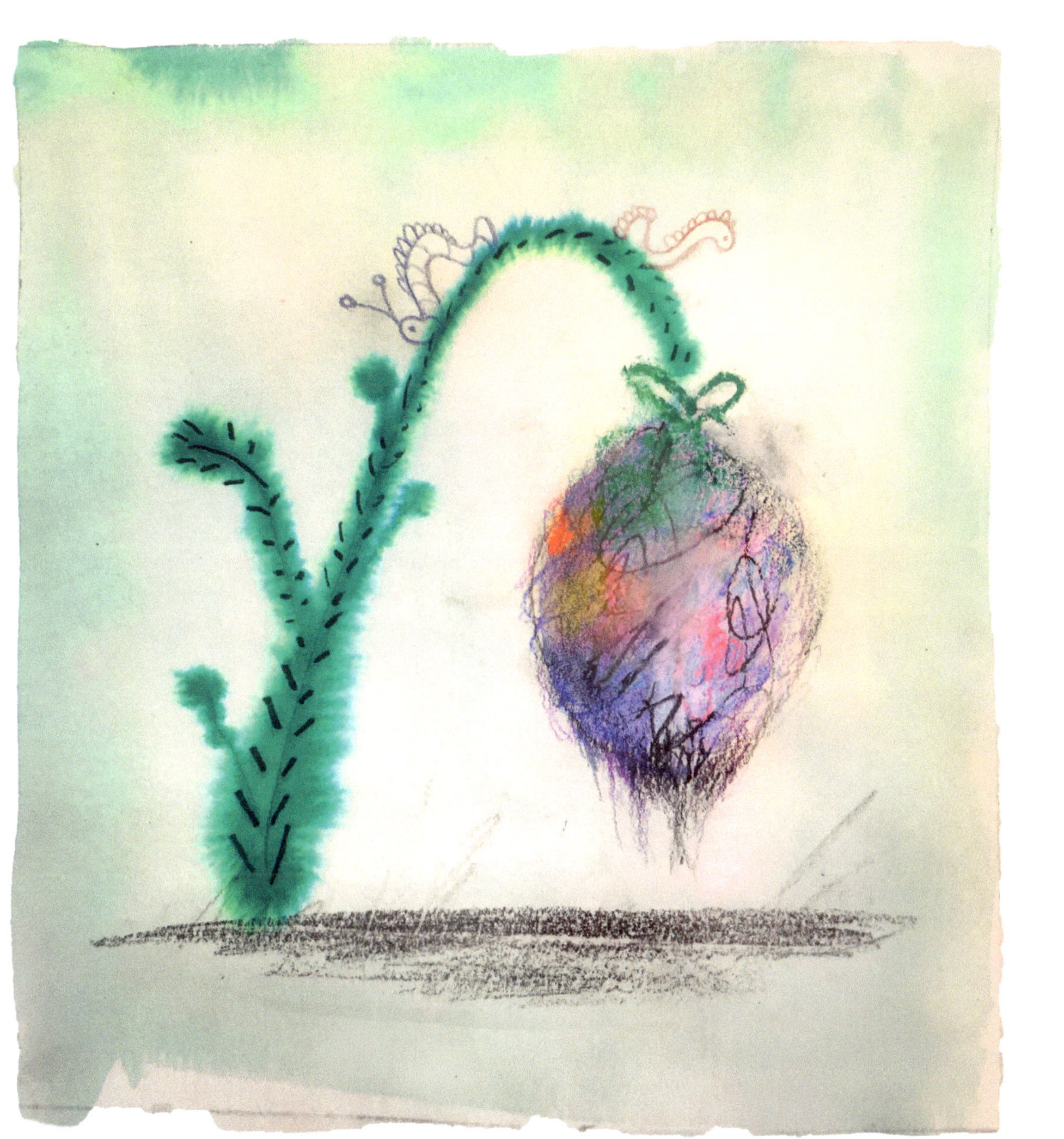

It looked up in surprise to see that the missing horn had grown back even bigger than before! Its drab beige spots were now as bright as the Sun.

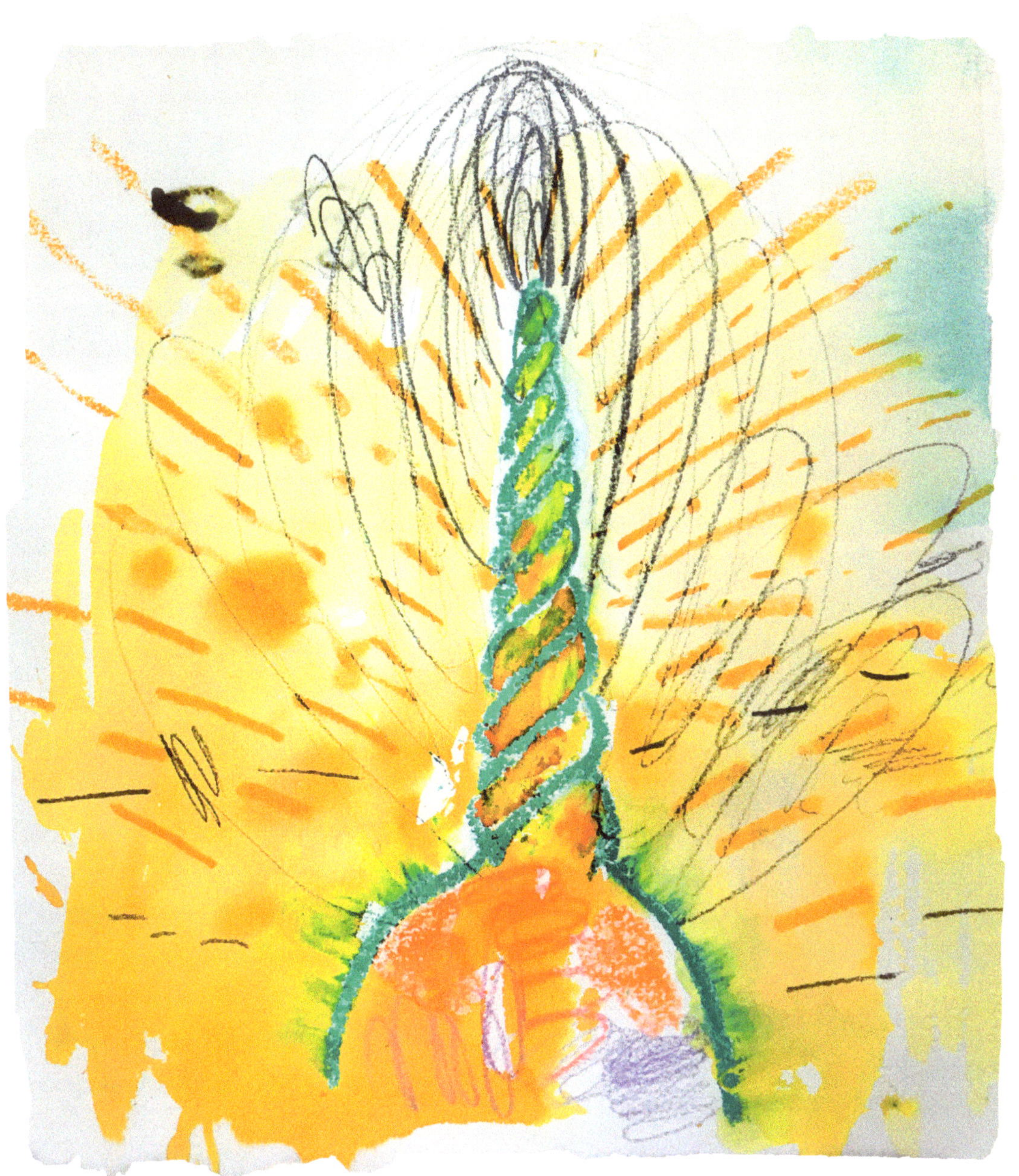

As the sleepy haze lifted, Ooni began to feel new feelings, see new colors,
and hear beautiful new sounds. It realized that these sparkling things had always been there;
it had just failed to see them before.

It no longer felt alone.

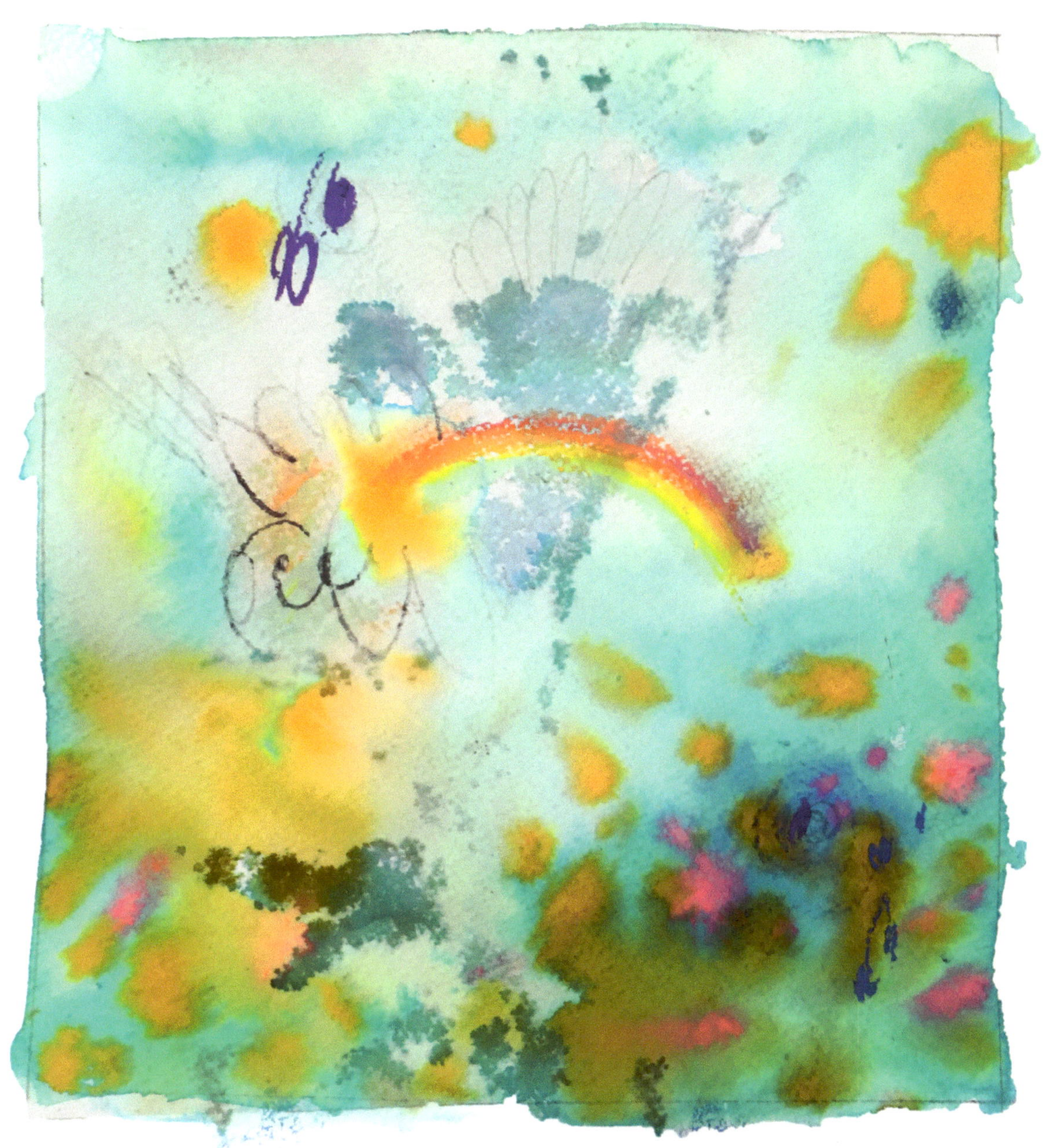

And, at last, it felt inspired to make thingies again! It really didn't know why.
And there may have been no point to any of it at all, other than that it filled Ooni's heart with joy.

A path appeared...

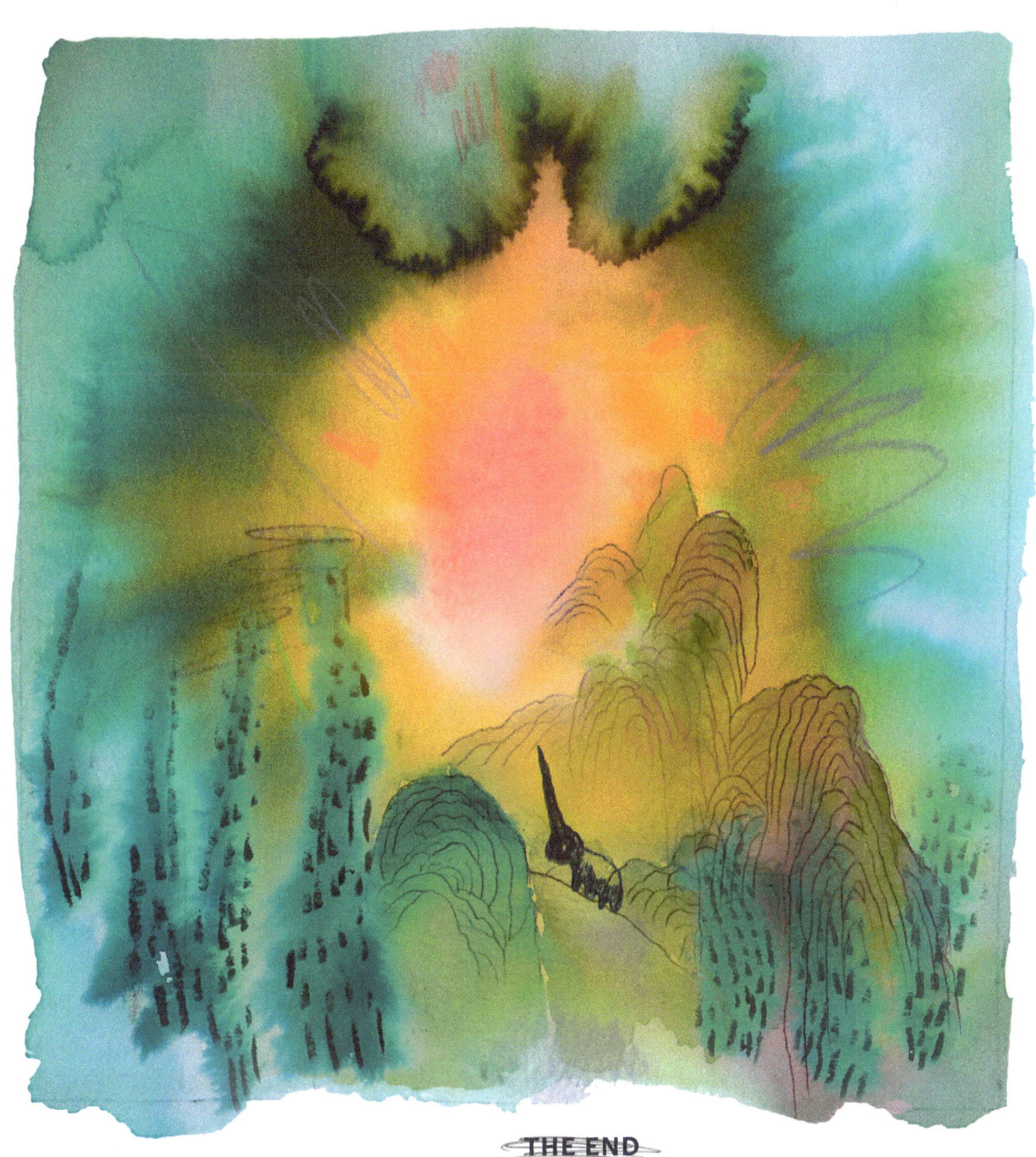

THE END

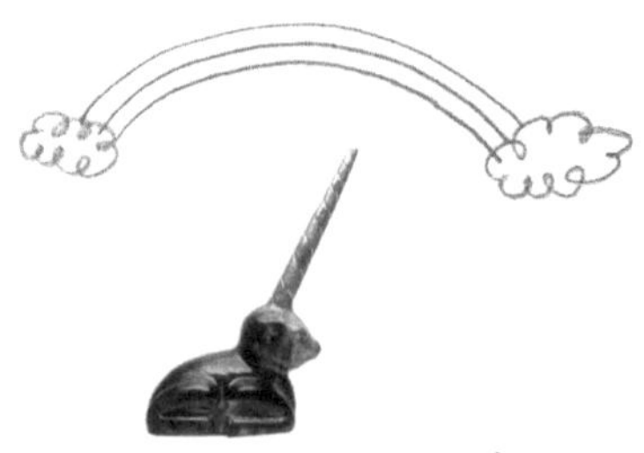

We are born with boundless imagination.

It begins as something free and flourishing but is oftentimes dimmed,
covered up, then cut off.

Following our heart is an ongoing process of unearthing inner worlds...
the "thingies" we create are the records of this journey.

Take the first step and a path appears.

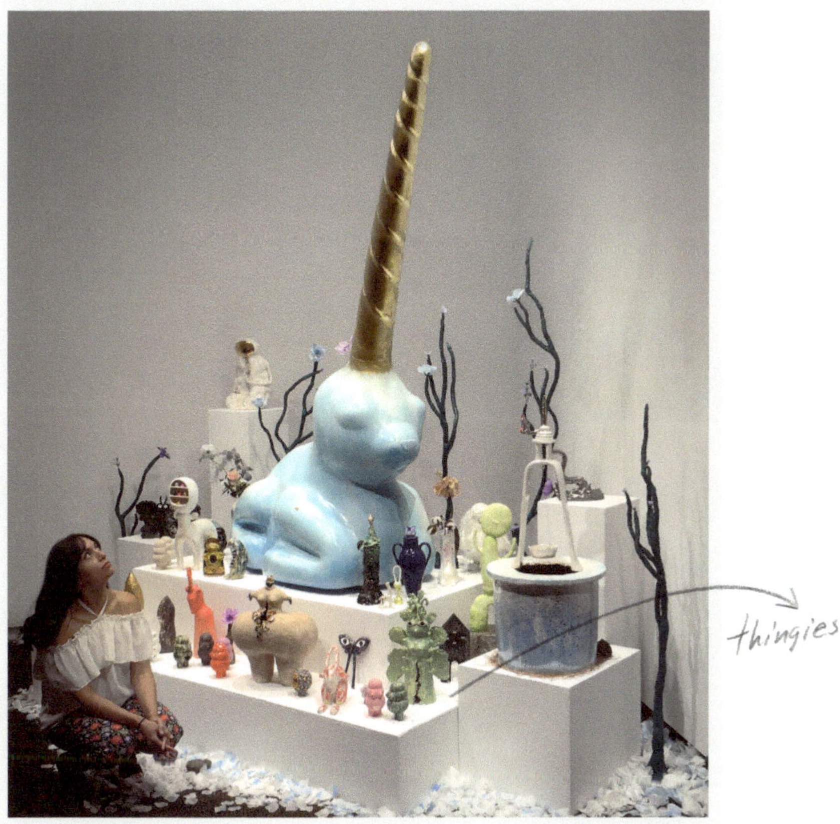

Shamona Stokes is an artist based out of Jersey City, NJ.

The image above is an installation of her sculptures entitled "Horn of Plenty",
which was exhibited at the Fort Worth Community Art Center in Texas (2019).
You can view more of her artwork at shamonastokes.com.

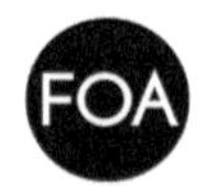

FRIENDOFTHEARTIST.COM

ISBN 978-1-64945-851-3

Thank you for reading my story.
* CREATED SEPTEMBER 2019 ♡

www.ingramcontent.com/pod-product-compliance
Lightning Source LLC
Chambersburg PA
CBHW042155030726
47599CB00004B/746